Esse's Self Denial Box

A Lesson of Self Denial

By Melissa M. Walker

Introduction

Children can learn from early on how important self denial is and how to live it day by day. Our human nature strives to put ourselves first. But, Jesus gives us lessons through his word , how it can be done through him and the joy it brings once it is accomplished. Every Christian home should have a Self-Denial box and should be taught to the children in early stages its importance.

One autumn day before worship, Esse and her mommy made a Self-Denial box for the family.

This box teaches the children to deny themselves of such unnecessary things as candies, gum, ice cream and other knickknacks, that they may put the money saved by their self-denial in the box. By this means large and small sums would be saved for the cause of God.

Our Self Denial

box

My Favorite Things

Little Esse learned in morning worship the necessity of how to deny herself and give to others.

During worship that morning, Esse asked, "Mommy, why do I have to be last?

Her mommy said, "Esse, our Savior Jesus Christ in Matthew 16:24 said, "If any man will come after me, let him deny himself, and take up his cross, And follow me."

Today, Esse revealed what she had learned.

Esse's cousin had come for a visit and she was about her age.

Mom decided to make wholesome pineapple muffins, she had made enough for everyone to have at least one.

While Esse and her cousins had been enjoying eachother's company, they also talked about how they could not wait to eat the delicious muffins her mother had baked!

Esse and Remy

Esse and her cousin Bella went into the kitchen to eat the muffins after they had finished playing.

But, to her surprise, when they arrived, there was only one muffin left.

You can imagine how they must have felt to see only one muffin left!

Esse thought about
the Self -Denial box.
So she walked over to
the kitchen drawer
and pulled out a sheet
of paper and a pen
and she wrote:

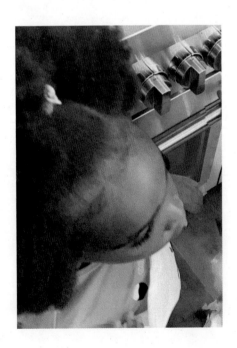

"Today, I will give Bella the last muffin".

Esse folded the sheet of paper, and placed it into the Self-Denial box.

When Esse saw her mommy later on that day her mother asked, "Esse, how did you enjoy the muffins?

Esse replied, "Mommy, there was only one muffin left, and I gave it to Bella to make her happy.

Esse's mommy hugged her tightly and said, "Jesus loves you very much, and He put Himself last, so that we may be first!"

THE END

For further information or copies, please send an email to

peacelily144@icloud.com

Thank you